Everything in Between

DEMI CHERYL

WESTBOW
PRESS®
A DIVISION OF THOMAS NELSON
& ZONDERVAN

Scriptures taken from the Holy Bible, New International
Version®, NIV®. Copyright © 1973, 1978, 1984, 2011 by
Biblica, Inc.™ Used by permission of Zondervan. All rights
reserved worldwide. www.zondervan.com The "NIV" and
"New International Version" are trademarks registered in the
United States Patent and Trademark Office by Biblica, Inc.™

WestBow Press books may be ordered through
booksellers or by contacting:

WestBow Press
A Division of Thomas Nelson & Zondervan
1663 Liberty Drive
Bloomington, IN 47403
www.westbowpress.com
1 (866) 928-1240

Because of the dynamic nature of the Internet, any web
addresses or links contained in this book may have changed
since publication and may no longer be valid. The views
expressed in this work are solely those of the author and do
not necessarily reflect the views of the publisher, and the
publisher hereby disclaims any responsibility for them.

Any people depicted in stock imagery provided by
Getty Images are models, and such images are
being used for illustrative purposes only.
Certain stock imagery © Getty Images.

ISBN: 978-1-9736-4356-2 (sc)
ISBN: 978-1-9736-4357-9 (hc)
ISBN: 978-1-9736-4355-5 (e)

Library of Congress Control Number: 2018912720

Print information available on the last page.

WestBow Press rev. date: 10/23/2018

What This Book is About

This book is the anthology of thousands of memories, presented as a collection of poetry. Entrenched in beauty, doused in pain, "Everything in Between" is the story of a hurting heart, pleading with a gracious God to find peace of mind and rest for the weary soul.

Dedication

I dedicate this book to the significant people in my life, you all know who you are. I dedicate this book to those who have made me work harder, struggle more and hurt frequently. This book is for you. But I truly dedicate this book to my family. To my Mom, who's had my back and been my cheerleader for years, thank you. To my brother who has continuously questioned and challenged me to be a better writer, sister and friend; thank you.

But, I could not even have thought about completing this book if it hadn't been for my Dad. To you Daddy, I want to say thank you. You have made me into the young woman I used to dream of being. You have held my hand even though I don't physically feel your touch anymore and you have walked me through.

By the grace of God, I've completed something, and it wouldn't have happened without you. Daddy, you are dearly missed, greatly loved and will never be forgotten. I will write about you, with you and for you until my dying breath. And then Daddy, I will run into your arms again.

Final Note

Thank you to the Lord of all creation for the breath in my lungs, the words which I pen and a voice to speak for those who won't. "I will go, Lord send me."

-Isaiah 6:8 MSG

"I remain confident of this: I will see the goodness of the LORD in the land of the living."

-Psalm 27:13 NIV

Part One:

―――――

The Darkness

This section deals with the downside of life. It is not pretty, not fun or funny and it gets real. But it is true. And I believe as many of you that there's always two sides to every story. Well, here are mine.

$\mathcal{C}$hapter 1

Mental health has been my biggest inspiration and struggle. After being diagnosed as bipolar I thought my life would improve. However, the challenges have only increased and I used this section to write about my failures and my frustrations surrounding mental health.

Things Unseen

Lurking in the shadows
Of my dark and depressed mind
Lie things I couldn't share with you
Even if I tried

I see faces, if you can call it that
Though twisted in proportion
I see colours that represent
My thoughts and their distortion

I'm not crazy, but I'm sick
And so, I take the happy pills
To try and stop the tears that I've been crying,
against my will

I sleep all day for fourteen hours
And then I take a rest
Cause nightmares are exhausting
Though I try to do my best

And then of course there's socializing
Of which there is no end
I'm always in a constant state of
panic with my friends

"Am I going to say something dumb?
Or will they embarrass me?"
It's not like I can take a break
From social anxiety

My moods are at best, unstable
Though I'm working through DBT
And I've seen five different counsellors
Who say there's "Nothing *wrong* with me"

On the outside looking in
I seem to have it all
But on the inside looking out
My own face I can't recall

I'm forgetful, lazy and self-centered
Just to name a few
But my Mom says I'm funny
So that, I guess, will do

The only reason that I shared this
Is to get you to try to see
That things aren't always what they seem
Especially, to me.

The War Within

Good and evil pull with in
I hear these voices
Telling me to stay or go
But they are both my own

It's hard to trust
When doubt is natural
And fear is all I know
The voices never go away,
I wake up and they're with me

At night they manifest themselves into
Images in my dreams
But when I wake they're but a screaming whisper
In my mind

They tear apart my sanity
And replace in me fatigue
Until I'm tired of fighting
And death is my only peace

With a slice of silver,
A flash of red appears
Boldly across my skin
Once and for all, all is calm
With the war within

An Attempt

Trying hard to fight these tears
Gasping for oxygen
So, I can take one final breath

Laying on the bedroom floor
Looking at what I have left
Cause I can't take it anymore.

A little bit of blood was all it took,
Just some blood for one last look
A longing gaze...I've been lying here for days

What's the use in hoping anymore
When it just gets you to the bottom
Where's my pain relief?

"End it all" "No one cares" Repeating in my mind
Not a word that's kind
Instead I feel the hatred boil up in my skin

Screaming out but there's no reply
Shouting for my last goodbye
Crying hard because no one hears my sigh

Panic Attack

Do you know what it feels like to have
hands slowly choke out the life inside
Squeezing the hope right out of your eyes
As fear rises and your body goes numb
You lose feeling in your mind as
your heart bleeds out
Letting go of your dreams, the hands get tighter
The room grows dim
Acceptance dawns that death is your fate
When do you realize that these
hands are...your own?

Ms. Understood

No one heard me
No one listened
No one saw me
No one was there
No one cared
No one helped
And when I cried, no one came
Tears of sadness
Tears of pain
Tears from the heart
Then someone came
Someone helped and heard my cry
Someone listened
Someone cared
Someone saw
Someone took the time
They hear me now

DEMI CHERYL

Anxiety

Her heart was willing
But her mind, afraid
So, when her heart said "GO"
Her mind screamed... "WAIT!"

A Weakness as Strength

"What's wrong with me?" She asks,
At only seven years of age.
She knew that she was different
Early on in this life stage

"What's wrong with me?" She repeats
Though this time she's had it rough
There really are voices telling her
She isn't good enough.

"What's wrong with me?" she cries
After another broken heart
She tries to stop the hurting
but that just makes the bleeding start

"What's wrong with me?" She yells
On the roof, floating in the air
If I were to fall to pieces
Would one single person care?

"What's wrong with me?" she survived
After jumping from the fall.
Looking around the room
She sees she's been loved all along.

"Nothing's wrong with you sweet girl,"
Come the praises pouring out
"You love deeply, feel strongly and give all of
yourself"
And darling, that's what life's about.

Heart-Breaking

Why's it gotta hurt so bad
Will it ever not be breaking
Cause I can't take one more breath

Why's it gotta be so hard
Wish I really was just faking
Cause I can't take another step

Why'd you have to cut me down
Now I know the truth that's in me
The ink on my skin is permanent

I can't face myself any longer
I can't even stand to see
Anyone looking at me

I feel like it's all my fault
One big joke and no one's laughing
Why'd you have to make a fool of me?

Wish it really could be different
Wish this wasn't just my life
But I can't crawl out of my skin

Could you please knock now darling?
My heart is opening
And I can't take another break

"Sweetheart, everything's okay now
Just let go you'll be alright"
I can see the love in your eyes

You only get this one life to live
You choose how you deal with it
As for me, I gave it my best shot

Finally, I can get my piece of rest
And now that I can let you go
I'm done, I gave it all I've got.

Chapter 2

This section was extremely difficult to publish, because it was so personal. I do not advocate for abuse nor do I condone it. However, I do understand it, so if these posts resonate with anyone please feel free to seek help or reach out. I am always in prayer for the hurt and abused.

The Art of Moving On

I spent a lot of time thinking;
About you, about me,
About what I could've done
Differently

I spent a lot of time crying;
Tears of loss, tears of pain
Tears that I would never get to
See you again

Then I spent some time moving;
Moving forward, moving on
Moving right to
Where I belong

Now that you're gone
It's plain to see, plain as can be
It's plain as day that you
Weren't meant for me

And so
Now I know
It goes to show
That sometimes moving forward means
Simply letting go

Fingers Crossed

I let you in, brought you into my home and let you into my heart. Listened to your sugar-coated lies. As you tell me I'm the only one, your fingers cross behind your back. Who's really to blame that I fell for your games? It's only me. The hardest part is recognizing that it's not just you. I fell for the fallacy too. I wanted to believe in us, in you. So badly that I held my breath and crossed my fingers too.

A Piece of Me

I wish I'd been able to tell you of, give you a piece of my mind. But why should you have both, a piece of my heart and my mind? You don't deserve that much of me. You're a coward and being the bigger person will only continue to make me stronger, so thank you. For making me brave. For giving me the courage to walk away from my abuse. And for helping me find out that my confidence doesn't lie in your opinion of me. No, I am confident because of who I *am.* Who you DID NOT destroy. And for that, you get no credit whatsoever. I am who I am in *spite* of you, not because of you. I think that what I need now is to get back to me. Not to lose myself in another person who's already lost themselves. I need to know who I was before you, and the fact that I'm living in confidence after is enough proof that I will be okay, but I don't know about you. I don't know that you ever were alright. Huh, too bad.

See, you inspired the worst in me. I was never my best self with you. I lacked motivation and purpose. But what I lacked in confidence, you helped me make up for in depression, and insecurity. Thank you for that. Why you felt the need to raise yourself up on the death of my dreams, I'll never know. But know it was unbecoming of you. I would've given anything for you. Too bad you couldn't do the same. So I let you go. Long before you ended things I had already let go of the image of us. In my heart I said goodbye to the piece of history that belonged to you and me. Our past, as finite as the love you once tried, but failed to give. The only thing left within, was the piece of me that I kept from you. Like a starfish regenerating a new limb, so I create my new self around the piece of me you didn't take. You don't get to win.

A Beautiful Mistake

I'm afraid I don't really love him. I'm afraid because I want to be loved so badly, but what if this is not meant to be? What if he isn't my everlasting always and forever? What if he's just a step to getting there. I'm scared he's right. That I might not be in love with him, but I want to be. I just don't know how; I'm afraid. I'm afraid that when I close my eyes this is real life but when I open them it was all a dream. And most of all I'm afraid that this is nothing more than a beautiful mistake.

Drowning Love

Love, save me from what I've become
I can't take back the things I've done
I'm sorry that I broke your heart
But, I'm trying not to fall apart

I've walked away a thousand times
Still I've never heard you say goodbye
Love, help me cause I've come undone
I'm afraid that what we had is gone

Love are you there or are you gone for good
Did you leave me like I knew you would?
You've taken my smiles and laughter too
Now all I've got are tears from you

Love, I'm drowning now and you're not near
Please tell me that someone else is here
Love, save me from my brokenness
I did it to myself, so let me go I guess

Love, I'm sorry that I messed this up
I'm still wishing I could make it up
To you because my intentions were true
But now, all I have are thoughts of you

DEMI CHERYL

Your Love

Your love is a big, black hole
I get sucked in by your pull
I'm falling through time and space
Pulled tighter by your embrace
I stay, because you say I'm beautiful.

Your love is a deep blue sea
I'm drowning in your reality
Tumbling through the raging waves
Struggling to breathe and be okay
I fight, because you say you love me.

Your love is a shadow at night
Surrounding me in plain sight
As frightening as it seems
I'm used to these schemes
I know, that everything is alright.

Your love is a tightly clenched fist
Or as I say, guilt with a twist
I'm broken and bruised
Worthless and used
But still, I don't get the gist.

Your love is a blood red slice
I conceal the pain with a bag of ice
The only way out that I can see
But when you say that you need me
I stay, I don't even think twice.

Broken Love

I'm broken and empty
You were the one who could've saved me
I grabbed your hand
But you let me go

Where were you when I lost it all?
How could you just sit there watch me fall?

It hurts to fall in love...
That's why they call it falling
Because when you hear love calling,
You fall and sometimes.... you break

$\mathcal{C}$hapter 3

On Justice

This section is close to my heart for many reasons. I've witnessed and experienced bullying, or hardships firsthand and it is a real trigger for me.

I try my best to treat people fairly and with justice, but I am always working on new and better ways to treat people. This section explores these themes amongst ways in which I have failed to measure up.

To The One

To the one who's been broken and used
To the one who has been hurt and abused

To the one who hides from the night
To the one who's afraid, too scared to shine bright

To the one who pretends because fake's all you know
To the one who is ready to start but won't go

To the one who is already over it
To the one who is scared that we can see through it

To the one who is forgotten, ignored or misplaced
To the one who is loved but cannot seem to find grace

To those who claim darkness over light
To those who are always ready to fight

To the one who is following but unsure
To the one who feels ashamed and impure

To the one who has captured the essence of life
To the one who has endured both toil and strife

To the one who belongs yet still wears a mask
To the one who feels like the only outcast

To the one who longs to be loved
To the one who always dreamed of

To each of the individual, hearts, minds and souls
Know that your value is innate, you are whole

Do not let your fears or failures hold you back
Do not let one mistake become a setback

To all of us fighting hard to let this truth be known
Your walk makes you shine, and the light is yours
alone.

Unnecessary

I've watched my spirit waste away
Night by night, and day by day
You think it's easy to be me?
To feel this shame? To face defeat?
I stand alone with my head low
Going through things that no one knows
You think you know me because of my past?
You never even tried to ask
Who I am
What I need
What I face
What I seek
You just assumed I'm incomplete
Because I'm broken and I'm weak
But what I have is quiet strength
To notice brokenness and pain
So, don't be mad if I don't care
About the slander that you share
I'm confident in who I am
I don't need your opinions...ma'am
So why don't you think twice before
You try and hurt me anymore

What's Wrong with the World Today

What's wrong with the world today?
What happened to the gentleman
He now steps upon lesser man
Because he truly thinks he "can...?"
What's wrong with the world today?"

What's wrong with the world today?
More gun fighting and sword fighting
Endings with broken-hearted "goodnighting" ...

What's wrong with the world today?

Why are there babies lying cold
Dank and dark inside a soul
Why's the homeless feeding homeless
While persecuted walk free?
Why's the adolescent's incessant chant about
"What is wrong with me?'

Oh Holy Ghost where is your antidote?
Give me poison, better yet, sing you're
Gracious melody.
Let me see beyond tomorrow
After yesterday's come through
I feel aware that I am nothing without you.

Give me liberty or give me death
There's no imperfect in between
So, Father, I glory to join You
As I share in Your victory

DEMI CHERYL

For you see,
This IS My Story.

So, Lord we're hurting and broken
And you are what the world needs today
So, Father hear my cries, and hear my prayers
And Father, just have your way.

A Leader

A leader is someone who stands up for the truth
In a world that is full of lies

A leader is someone who gives their all
In a world where nobody tries

A leader is someone who smiles each day
In a world that is filled with deception

A leader is someone whose vision is clear
in a world with distorted perception

A leader is someone who is not afraid
To stand up for someone in need

A leader is someone who loves a challenge
Determined at all costs to Succeed.

A leader is someone who gives sound advice
When counsel or input is sought

A real leader leads with love and integrity
And treasures the blessings they've got

A leader is someone who values the beauty
In simplistic things everyday

A leader is someone who knows how to step down
And not always do things their way

DEMI CHERYL

In a world that is fallen and aging in time
We are in need of something new
Let yourself fight for a change worthy cause
And reveal the true leader in you.

Chapter 4

The most difficult thing in the world for me is how to put into words how much I love someone who is no longer here. My Dad was a great man of God and not only raised me with love but taught me through his actions and the integrity he had. He showed me how to be loved and treated with dignity and respect. This whole book is a dream come true birthed from early conversations with my dad.

Thank you, Daddy for being what a real gentleman, father and role model should be.

After All

I didn't know that my life would be divided into two parts; before and after. I didn't think that you wouldn't see my happily ever after or my forever and always. I didn't know. Before, it was, well it's simple really, you were mine. And I was always supposed to be yours. That's all it needed to be. I was going somewhere. And you were where you always were; here with me.

Before, you were my favourite person. You made me mad, happy; you were like the remote controller of my emotions. Everything I ever felt was because of you, and I guess that's the same for after too.

But before you taught me how to love and be loved. You taught me it's okay to laugh at myself. You taught me that I'm okay just as I am and that it's okay to make mistakes. Before, I didn't know that I had more to look forward to in life. You changed me for the better and made me what I am today. I'd like to think I'm better anyways. But that was all before.

Everything was the way it always was, I didn't know there was a before. But there was, because I'm living in after.

After, my heart hurts every day and reminding me of the constant feeling that I'm missing something. Or in this case, you. After, I wake up feeling dead inside and I know I can say that because it's true. You kept me alive and you kept me dreaming of a future, my future. A future that was supposed to have you in it.

My wedding, my kids, my graduations, they were all supposed to include you, you had to be there. But that was before. Before we had plans, or at least I did. I had dreams and you were my encourager. Before you, I didn't know that I could feel anything this badly but after, it's like all my senses are stimulated at once and they're all pulling me in different directions. I feel so much all the time, that for once I'd just like to feel nothing at all. I guess that's why I do it now. Because after you, it helps silence the screaming pain that pierces through my heart.

I wish sometimes that I'd never met you. That you'd never been a part of my life. Not because I hate you, no not at all. Quite the opposite actually, I love you more than I love myself. I love you more than anyone I've ever loved. And it's not fair that I have to live in after, without you. Because before, well that's easy, you were here, and we were us.

After is all memories, all photographs, and all of me missing all of you.

Polite Ignorance

When something life-altering happens in your life, something earth-shattering, you can truly see the way that people change around you. They get awkward or skittish, they whisper around you and fake smile because your loss makes *them* uncomfortable.

When my dad died, people looked at me like I was broken, and they could see the tear.

Ironically there was one, but I didn't like people staring at it. I remember the people who, with pure pity in their eyes, stood around and told me "I'm sorry for your loss." As if their insincere apologies meant anything at all to me.

Nonetheless, I digress, when something terrible happens it's strange the way that people treat you. It's also funny the way you start to treat yourself. I found myself caving into my soul repressing my feelings and retreating so that I could

only be found in the walls of my books and the journals of my soul.

The strangest thing that happens when you lose someone you love, is that people simply care until the next big thing. People don't have the time to care or give effort into pretenses when they are busy living and loving their own lives. And so they forget… They stop caring because it no longer affects them.

And that's the long and short of it. You don't care, and you don't have to care. Why should you? It didn't happen to you.

Cycle of Grief

What if loss is all I get
What if I cannot forget
What if there's no other way
Then losing you to all this pain

Day by day I see myself
Slowly slip away
What if one day I lose it all
And you're no longer there

Take these hands and bind them
So, I can no longer feel
I am captive to my loss
And I no longer care

You are gone, and you have left me here
Without so much as a mop
To wipe up the bloodshed that we've made
And heal the scars that cannot fade

All hail the one who's in heaven now
But woe to us on earth
The life cycle shall continue
With life...then death... then new birth.

DEMI CHERYL

For You

For you I'd give a thousand dollars even if I had none
For you I'd fight a dragon though it's impossible to find one

For you I'd ride against the night by taking on the sea
For you'd I'd become president so that one day you'd be proud of me

Your being gone changed my whole world with the departure of a hearse
But without you every single thing hurts and it progressively gets worse

I cry myself to sleep at night wishing I could just see you.
And when I wake up in the morning I wish that I could keep you

I didn't know how much you had impacted my whole life
Until you're no longer in it do I start to realize

So for you dear dad, I'd climb the peak of Everest just to see you.
For you my father I hope that heaven is perfect enough for you.

Without you I am a lost citizen just passing through world

But for you my dad, my hero, I'm still your Baby Girl.

Everything In Between

There is no other earthly pain
That compares to losing you
No broken heart could measure up
My joy and hope withdrew

You live in my memories
but you've died in my heart
I don't see your face or feel your warmth
Now that we are apart.

I wish that things were better
I wish that you were still here
Because when I close my eyes at night
You are.... then you disappear.

It's not that you don't love me
I know that you always cared
it's simply the fact that I don't know
how to live when you're not here

I loved you most with all my heart
My mind and my soul too
So, Daddy when I say this
Just know that it is true

You are my sunshine in the sky when I feel blue

You are the night light in the moon when I can't
even feel you

You are the whispers in the wind, you are the things unseen

And Daddy, my sweet father you're my everything in between.

Part Two:

Light

In this section you'll find my reflections on the "good" in life. Years of memories and hard work but also the joys of loving, laughing and living with the ones I love.

$\mathcal{C}$hapter 5

"Give me something to believe in"

I've filled these pages with my hopes and dreams as well as fears and trials and how my faith in God helps me overcome my hinderances.

The Peak

In the valley of the shadow of death
I will keep on singing until my dying breath
I can see mountains around me on all sides
But I lift my head and look to the skies

I'm calling on Heaven
To fight my battles
I'm calling on love
To win this war
I'm crying out in mercy
For the pain, tears and scars
I'm calling on Jesus to restore

The valley may be where we are
But it isn't where we stay
Look up to the mountaintops,
Deliverance is on the way.

Though the enemy stares me down
Evil grins with earthly crown
I will face the cross and wait
Because my Jesus saves

I'm calling on Hope
To plant a garden
I'm calling on Peace
To calm the seas
I'm calling on faith
To intervene, like I knew you would
And I'm answering Your call of me

Jesus put me in the valley to
To teach me who I am
And from that darkened valley
I became the me that can

So I'm holding my ground until I get there
I'm not going down so don't push me
So you can hate me or berate me
But nothing can keep me down, you'll see

I'm standing on Jesus blood
He shed for me, he gave his life
For my story, so I could climb out of the pit
And look a top of all of it.

So I could be a lamp
Unto the darkest streets
To shower grace and mercy on
My enemies

So that I may bear witness
To the Power I've received
To love like Jesus loved me...
From the mountain peak.

Choose

Breathe you out
Just to breathe you in
Let you go
Just to fall again
How many times
Will I lose before I win?

Faith is waning,
Hope unsure
Love is lost
My hearts impure
How can I still be called
Your own?

You call me chosen
I feel that I'm broken
You say I am loved
I say "Not good enough"
You scream the loudest whisper
"I am yours".

But what makes the difference
from faith to existence
What calls me out
Of this darkness I live in

What is this light-beam shining over me?
How do I know I can trust what I see?
Are you another person that can hurt and
betray me?
Or is this the real love I've been craving?

Tell me so I choose
either love or abuse
Because I'm tired of the pain
I just want to be whole again

So, if the promise is made
And I can truly be loved
Then I choose Faith, Hope and Love
So, I can live the life I dream of.

He Says

I tell Him I won't
That I don't want to fail
He says its ok
That with Him I'll prevail

I tell Him I'm not
But I wait for Him to say
That I am, and I will be
In every possible way

I tell Him I don't
And my heart falls apart
But He tells me he does
And He heals my broken heart

I tell Him I can't
I won't even try
He tries to convince me
That I will, and I cry

I tell Him I can't
I don't know what I'm about
He tells me "You can"
With a firm, heartfelt shout

He tells me "You will"
With a passionate cry
But I ask Him how
Too much time has gone by

He tells me "You are"
And He says it with pride
I ask Him how come?
But I'm beaming inside

He tells me "He loves me"
And I know that it's true
For the first time ever
I say, "I do too"

Ink in My Veins

Through these tears I cry
Let them know your name
With these words I pray
Let them learn of your Fame

If I hurt with nothing left
Let that be my story
But it's worth it if this feeble heart
Can bring you Glory

Take these shaking hands
And teach them how to write
Words worth reading
Leading, and learning to live right.

If I die because I've loved you
Then my death won't be in vain
I hope to love and love well
Though my life is filled with pain

I hope my life is used for good
Because if not, then what's it all worth?
What good is to breathe new breath
And still see a world of hurt

If I can't impact one single life,
Then I've failed in every way
My life was made to lose not gain
But to simply give away

With these words I pen my heart
Pour blood out on this page
The ink I bleed is poison
Beneath my youthful age

My skin is marked by slices
Scars both old and new
Because I bleed for my heart
But I mostly bleed for you

This is where I leave you now
The time has finally come
If life has taught me anything it's that
If you make it to the end then...you've won

Your Light

Does your light forbear to shine?
When darkness ceases to exist
Just because other's shine around you
Doesn't mean your light is not missed
Shine bright dear darling, and let your light be seen
For you're as bright as the sun, the moon
And everything in between

$\mathcal{C}$hapter 6

"Someday"

Hope is something I've struggled with for the past seven years. With loss and heartache Hope is something that I've chosen to believe in. Simply because there has to be a reason to see beyond my circumstances. I have to trust in something bigger then myself because this life has to mean something.

To Be like Her

"Oh how she knew how brief this life could be, for she knew just how instantly a life could be taken from us. Yes she knew how short a life could be, that's why she spent every moment looking upward. For she had heaven in her eyes."

"She wasn't the type of girl to run scared from anything, she'd simply reach out and caress the beast and it would melt like putty into her delicate fingers. With one glance, she could melt hail and turn ice into rain. She was brave in a bold way yet she needn't have to say a word. She was a gentle spirit; a quiet soul. And that is why they hated her for it. Because there was no one like her and because there would never be."

"She was the most beautiful when she cried. When raw emotion poured from her and her heart leaked through her eyes. She thought that no one saw for she'd wipe her tears quietly and in haste. But He saw her. And He knew what to do best. He was always aware of her tears. For it was when they were all wiped and neatly tucked away that he'd collect them. Store them up for her in a clay jar. Yes he knew when she cried. He always knew. And it was the brokenness in her that was most beautiful to Him."

Caught in Death's Headlights

There's bomb quickly beating;
Inside your chest.
Time slowly ticking away.
As you watch life after life wasting their days.

There's a tomb with your name on it.
It's ok mine's there too.
And when you finally hear Death's trains' whistle.
A train goes passing through.

Your heart speeds up.
"Ok now is my time"
But the trains pass through so fast.
You can't tell if your dead or alive.

"Are you kidding me?"
You yell, because you can.
But can you take away a life
That's part of God's plan.

I truly believe in miracles
Why? Because I'm living proof.
I used to spend every day wondering
Am I good enough for you?

Let them Speak

Let the words flow freely from my heart to my pen
Let them tell of the depths of the pain that I'm in
Let them speak of despair and of heartbroken love
Let them tell of the darkness that I still dream of
Let them write of the losses
that still grieve my soul
Let them ring of the hurt that has taken its toll
And let them speak of the truth that pain brings
New life to all broken and decaying things

Wonder

I've lost it all
Chasing after anything but you
So let me know where I can go
To have hope restored be renewed

I've wanted to be somewhere I'm not
My whole life has been
A chase for what's been forgotten

What's being missed in our world
the beauty in every day
I've lost the aesthetic eye
That I just gave away

I'm at my wit's end
I have nowhere else to go
Give me peace and show me
what it looks like to have Hope

Fill me with a sense
Of peace and prosperity
Open my eyes to the things
I have to gain by living free

And lastly let me be filled with
With fresh hope so I can willingly
Go, join in and see all
The wonder that's to be seen

DEMI CHERYL

Eyes of Light

Are we just kidding ourselves?
Looking for the answer in shards of broken glass
Are we just wasting our lives?
To be victims of grace but never truly whole

Are we ever satisfied with receiving
more useless things?
Or are we so tired of running in
circles that we just fall down.
That's how it was for me...

Sinking deep beneath reality
Face up I nearly drown
When I see your blinding light
Sweep me off the ocean ground

I reach for all you're showing me
Stretching my hands to yours
Gasping and sputtering for breath
You wrap your arms around me
And still you call me yours

You condition me with Grace
While washing mercy over me
And in my despair of outward shame
You allowed me to just to be.

Who I am and who you've made
Are synonymously unique
Both words essentially mean,
The world needs more of me

I won't shy away from the task at hand
I know my mission is clear
Live hard, Love harder
And fight fairly for the lesser man
Who's lost without a saviour

As for me, I do not always see you
when I lay back for a swim
But I feel you in the warmth of
sunlight that I've been buried in
Now darkness comes upon me like
a thief who wants my soul.
But emerging out of holy water he
sees that every scar is whole.

$\mathcal{C}$hapter 7

"The One I Loved Most...."

Love is probably my favourite thing to write about. I love the idea of falling in love and also the promise of staying in love. I myself only know the love I've written about but that doesn't mean I don't dream it and write it to the best of my ability.

Hello

When I see bright stars in broad daylight just know it's because I'm thinking of you. When I hear music in the dead of night it reminds me just how great my admiration is for you. When the moon smiles down at me after being out for hours, I smile back knowing that he knows my secret. The sun on the other hand, burns brightly, shining so that every shadow disappears in its way, letting everyone know the truth. I'm not ready to utter those words though everyone around me knows it.

I hesitate because, I don't know if you want to embark on this journey with me. And I'm so tired of being alone. Still I will ask, push past the fear, and open my mouth to say..." hello". For I can't do it, I chicken out every time. Just know behind every hello there's an "I Love You" that wishes to be spoken.

For the words I hear over and over and yet still I can't say, I'm sorry. If this life is about being brave and loud, bold and "out there" then this world has no place for me. Because I'll never tell you how I feel just because I feel it. I may utter some emotion under my breath. But until you tell me where you stand, just know that I am here, waiting to be loved by you. And so at least I know that I love you. You can stay oblivious or uninterested. I don't care. Right now, I know I love you and that's enough for me.

But know it's there, in the sparkle of your crooked smile, the pitch of your laugh when it comes from your stomach. The way you look, genuinely look people in the eyes when you talk to them. I didn't make up this love for you, it grew. Born out of a dream it grew, planted, potted and watered and then raised up to the sunlight. This love grew out of the kindness in your soul. If you knew how much this love has shaped me, made me believe and hold me accountable. If you truly knew how amazing, you are then everyone would love you too.

And I think in some ways they do know. I think that's why "we" can never become us. Because the world knows about you, sweetheart, and they adore you. But nobody knows about me. Nobody cares that I cared for you long before the flashy cars and flashing lights. I knew your name when no one bothered to look it up. And now...I'm afraid it's too late to show you my love. You've gone and got yourself another who will love you in ways I may never be able to. And it's ok because you deserve the world. Just know I wish you well, and maybe next time I see you...I'll say "Hello".

What if...?

What if the only way to receive was to let go?
What if saying goodbye was the way to a hello?
What if, to feel your warmth I had to stand out in the cold?
What if losing you was the only way that I could hold...
Onto my heart, onto my dream, onto this strange reality.

What if telling you how I feel means things are left unspoken?
What if truly loving you means that my heart gets broken?
What if having one more day means losing years together?
What if this one moment here and now is our forever?

What if I give all I am to find there's nothing left?
What if losing here and now makes me somehow the best?
What if I could have one wish, one dream that could come true?
.... What if God answered all my prayers with the gift of you.

A Thought

You could say that it's on me
Because I know that I fall hard
But does that mean I should be
Sorry for catching you off guard?

Is it really my mistake for
Simply loving you?
Am I really the one at fault
Because my heart was true?

It's hard for me to fathom
Why you've taken such offence
To be quite honest you should be flattered
Being mad, doesn't make sense

I'm not sorry though, for how I feel
It's not something I've mistaken
I'm sorry that I put a heart
In hands that will just break it

I'm sorry that you can't handle
Being valued and even wanted
But it's not my fault you've chosen
To see this as something daunting

You don't know love or even know
How To let yourself be free
But that is not my problem
I didn't ask you to love me

To accept my love is all I need
For I need to be real
Because I think that we both know
I can't control how I feel

You think I want to feel this way?
You think that this is fun?
Believe me I'd enjoy much more
For all of this to be done

You don't have to say a thing
There's nothing for you to do
But if you're feeling mature enough
Just own it, and say: Thank you.

A supposition

If your love was just a dream
I'd live my life asleep
Succumbing to the subconscious
Swallowed whole by the darkness

If your love was a river
I'd sink beneath the water
Let the air escape my chest
Holding on 'til my last breath

If your love was the sunlight
I'd live under the sky
Feel the brush of heat against my skin
Let the warmth of you sink in

If your love was a continent
I'd travel the world to live in it
Immerse myself in your culture
Knowing I'd live a life of adventure

If your love was the air I breathe
Than your literally all I'll ever need
I breathe you out; I'll breathe you in
Let you blow across my skin

Secret Hearts

Would you do it all again for me,
Knowing I wouldn't be around

Would you still be my friend?
Even though I let you down

Could you even love me?
Because it's too hard now

Because I can barely love myself
And loving you is unplanned

But I do, in my heart of hearts
See us hand in hand.

The secrets spilling like fairy tales
I see us; You...then Me

If I were to let you in
You'd see my transparency

So, my dreams stay hidden
My pride afraid
I can never let it show

Why?
Because, if you saw my secret heart
Well..., then darling you'd know.

A Broken Heart

A broken heart doesn't ever really
feel like a broken heart.
Your heart doesn't shatter it doesn't
crumble or crash. It's not over in an
instant or even in a moment.
It's not even so much the breaking
that's the problem.
When your heart falls... it breaks. The
falling is the act of inducing pain.
Whether your heart's has been thrown
around or dropped the instant that the
organ dislocates from your body searing, gut
wrenching pain seeps into your body filling
the heart shaped hole that was left behind.
A broken heart doesn't ever really
feel like a broken heart.

DEMI CHERYL

Just A Guy

You are just a guy
Not the first but not the last
Just number 5 in a list of guys
Who broke me in the past

You are just a guy
Nothing special; nothing more
Whatever else you choose to be
Doesn't matter anymore

You're not my prince or dream come true
So, you don't get to care
You're just another guy
Who chose to not be there

With you I wasted endless tears
I shouldn't have even shed
Because I knew exactly
How this starts and how it ends

It starts with hope filled little me
Believing you're the guy
Who's come to sweep me off my feet
And wipe the tears I've cried

It starts with dates and holding hands
And dreams of what will be
And shared secrets dancing upon
The lips of you and me

The faintest bit of magical
Electricity
When you kissed my lips with empty
Promises you couldn't keep

Yes it may have started well
As it often does
But the petals have since wilted
Off the stems of broken love

So it ends with silence filling up
The space between us two
I'm left with all the emptiness
Of not being enough for you

Because you're just a guy
This is how it'll always go
My hopes held high but my heart crushed
By what I should've known

Loving you

You woke me with your kiss
And I haven't slept since
I've come alive at your touch
Now I ache for your love
You don't care to see
That your love is killing me
But darling, loving you is
A bittersweet memory

The Waiting Game

Are you waiting for me?
As far as the mind can tell
As far as the eye can see?
Are you waiting for me?

Are you waiting for me?
To have and to keep
And to dream with while I sleep
Are you waiting for me?

Are you waiting for me?
Praying to God above
That I'll be the one you love
Are you waiting for me?

Are you waiting for me?
If time was to stand still
And empty lives were left to fill,
Are you waiting for me?

Are you waiting for me?
Countless hours spent without you
But even more spent missing you too
Are you waiting for me?

Are you waiting for me?
Or is your patience wearing thin
Because if so I understand but
Please don't hurt me again.

DEMI CHERYL

Are you waiting for me?
Cause if not don't waste my time
I'll wait for you 'til forever
But this time now mine

I'm waiting for your messages
I'll stop hoping that you'll call
I'm so busy living
I'd rather not know at all

So please wait or don't wait but
The decision isn't mine
Simply know, That I would wait
For you until the end of time.

The End

At the end of it all,
I'm just a girl who thought of loving you

At the end of the day,
You're just the guy who didn't want me to.

Over and over our hearts beat
to the sounds of broken dreams

Nothing will ever be the same
For nothing is as it appears to be

At the end of it all,
I'm just a girl who put it all on the line

At the end of the day,
You were the guy I hoped would be mine.

Over and Over our hearts bleed
To the sound of a thousand cries

Nothing will ever be new again
For how can, we move past these soul-ties

At the end of it all,
I'm just a girl full, from loving you

At the end of the day
You're just the guy that never knew

DEMI CHERYL

Chapter 8

This last section of the book tells what I know in my heart to be true. This is where I express the truths I know about myself and others. Whether or not you agree with what I say here, this is what I believe.

Dear One

It breaks my heart to know you're hurting this badly.
Would you let me take the pain away?

For I know the plans I have are worth having?
Can I make it all OK?

Dear One, just know your life is a good one?
Don't be sad today.

I see your tears and hear your prayers
But this is what I want to say.

I love you more than you could ever know
My love's been places you'll never go

You're free from all debtors and free from all pain
I've liberated you from all guilt, fear and shame

You have hope now and a new reason for being
And I am the breath in the lungs that you're breathing

Take heart, be still and have peace
Knowing there's rest when you come and find me

Relax and be still; take the edge off
You're not going anywhere that I have not gone

Walk close with me and you'll be safe
Don't go anywhere that I haven't Okayed

You're safe now, I'll be your anchor
Tether yourself to me and I'll stay closer

Rest well you're not in control anyway
Just wait 'til you see what I've got planned for today

My love, you're more than good enough
You are whole and perfect and deserving of love

I know that you'll fail you're human I know
But that's why I've called you, I've paid what you owe

Know that you mean everything to me
I have scars in my hands to prove your worthy

All that I ask, my simple request
Is to remember I died so that you could find rest

Remember me in your heart and keep your eyes on mine
And just watch the magic of our journey unwind

Dear one, there's just one thing left to do,
Let go of control and see what I have for you.

Take a deep breath I know this is hard
But know that I'm with you and I'll be your guard

Will you take this chance to walk by my side?
I know where you are I see where you hide.

Trust me Dear One nothing can touch you
If I haven't ordained it, then there's nothing it
can do

It's not now or never, but now would be good
For me to love you the way no man could

I just want to hold you, Dear One let me in
I have already chosen to forgive all your sin

It's time now to let go, just hold onto my hand
And get ready to embark on this journey I've
planned

Dear Fear

Here I am again, held down by your lies that I'm not good enough to try
To be anything other than captive to your cowardly lies
Fear you don't get to break me anymore I refuse
You can take back your deception and all other tactics you use

Fear you're a goner and I'm coming for your head
You made me think I was better off dead
You stole days I can never get back
You made me think I was wrong with every sneak attack

I don't want you here anymore fear get lost
I am done with you I don't care what the cost
Your days are numbered so start the countdown
I want you to feel the very same frown

And I want you to remember you lose
I have Love on my side and I get its power to use
Love wins in the end fear don't you get that
You're nothing more than an insignificant gnat

You're all out of tricks your show is done
And you came out the loser, because I won
I don't believe in you anymore
Your power is unsure

You can't torment me when I know the truth
about you
You're less than nothing, you have no value
Truth is I've got the best of you
And now there's absolutely nothing you can do.

Weird

It's weird going back to where you started from;

Weird bad: because this is the reason so many tears were shed
Weird bad: knowing that so many people got hurt here
Weird bad: because there's nothing you can do to change history

It's also weird going back to where you start from;

Weird Good: Knowing that out of this place of darkness history was born
Weird Good: Because resilience and determination were breathed into existence
Weird Good: Knowing that history repeats itself and so we know that out of pain hope will rise.

It's always weird going back to where you're from.

Dear Princess

I used to want to be a princess as a little girl. I thought princesses were beautiful and I wanted so badly to be beautiful too. But I was never chosen to be a princess. Not once. I was the comedic sidekick. And so I learned that if I was funny, I got laughs and laughs meant that people liked me. So I would say the most outrageous things and not crack a smile. People would laugh and I would feel good... for a minute. But deep down I still wanted to be the princess.

Then, I used to want to have a knight come save me from "what I'm not too sure", but now I want to be that knight. Head in the war, heart in the trenches. I want to fight, for the lost girls trapped thinking they *need* a man to save them. Save them from what?

Darling daughters of Eve, save yourselves. You were not created for the sidelines. You bring the whole world down on it's knees when you bow.

You're mighty and strong. Do not make less of the gifts you've been given. Nor should you forget the power that's within you to be fearlessly beautiful and unimaginably unashamed.

No, see I used to want to be a princess, not anymore. Now, I'm in the war.

About the Author

Demi Cheryl is a twenty-four-year-old, Ontario native and has dabbled in writing for ten years. Having minor accomplishments over that timeframe, this is Demi's first attempt at writing a full-length book. Demi Cheryl's hobbies include, reading fiction (preferably Young Adult and Poetry), scrapbooking, going to movies with her friends and spending time with her family. Demi is also finishing her undergraduate degree.

CPSIA information can be obtained
at www.ICGtesting.com
Printed in the USA
LVHW040459011218
598878LV00001B/20

9 781973 643562